HomeWords

Poems and Prayers

By Jack Perkins

Moosewood Editions is proud to present this, the fifth book of poetry by Jack Perkins

© 2016 by Jack Perkins
Moosewood logo by MJ Designs

Soon available as an audiobook, poems read by author at audible.com

Follow author on Facebook - jackperk
Twitter - @jackperk
email: jackperk@jmac.com

Comments and orders for signed copies welcomed at:
orders@jackperkins.com

Also by author:

Parasols of Fern (with Mary Jo Perkins)
Acadia: Visions and Verse,(Poetography)
Island Prayers (Poetography)
Finding Moosewood, Finding God
Nature of God
Marveling (Poetography)
Sunrise Psalms

HomeWords

HomeWords tell of urgent questings,
Beings in search of a place uncertain,
Perhaps by springing from sand where a mother unknown
Deposited then abandoned them
Until this night when up they erupt
Knowing only enough to be going
On their own to where they need to go
Through the dark toward the light that bathes the sea
What draws them?
What, one day, will draw them back to this, their natal beach?
Home!
The urge to find and, sometimes, re-find home,
It's the strongest goading there can be —
For turtles — as for you and me.

In this life heading toward the next,
Let HomeWords move us ever homeward.

Jack Perkins

Dedicated to all who not only believe
but live their beliefs

Confession

Why do I write poetry? I don't.
I confess without shame
That of poems here I may seem to have written,
Many I only transcribed from incoming transmissions.

Sometimes at the first rays of dawn, they come;
Sometimes in the raven dark of night.
Sitting in the quiet of my room,
Tracking an ibis across a beach,
Embraced by the heart of a shaded wood,
Maybe in church a sermon or prayer lights a spark,
A word or phrase illuminate.
Maybe while watching a ball game an insight will materialize.
My body might be fighting infection
So my mind, evading pain, harks to signals.

Thus it happens. That is my role.
Enough to warrant my name on a book?
Let it at least be acknowledged
I never disclaim the Original Author
While serving as amanuensis,
Setting down insights entrusted to me.

The Holy Spirit does not have an iPad; I do.
God's voice is rarely heard. Mine is His to use.

Crafting gifted insights into verse takes workmanship, yes.
And the Greek word for "workmanship" is
Poema

Back Story

A poet needs to write himself.
Thus, he needs to know himself.
Both the now and then of him.

I have a back story,
Used to be this, used to do that,
So what?
I rollicked in the times of my past;
I regret them not.
But past has passed.
Its only value to me now
— As awards and recordings are long put away,
Clippings and plaudits yellowed —
Is that perhaps what I was and what I said
When I had nothing important to say
May accord me a whisper of echoed attention
Now that I do.
Now that I have the most important story
I have ever had to tell,
Most powerful news, and sorely needed;
I pray that any who heard me then
Will hear me now.
My news now is old yet I promise,
It is ever-new.

Rumor

So who am I?
A rumor,
Whispered but unverified,
Subject to serial speculation,
Never proved.

At times, to tell truth, I'm not even a rumor,
Scarcely the shadow of one,
Less than a figment,
An undefined word,
Vagary blurred,
A mirage, a chimera,
The memoir of things I wish had happened or would,
Written by the person I'd like you to think I am.
A frail tissue of tales, my rumorous memoir,
Offered as true and maybe so but maybe not,
By now the writer himself isn't sure
Nor does he care;
Content is he to be but rumor.
After all, if he does not yet know himself,
Why should anyone else?

Jack

My parents named me Jack,
Hastening to tell me and all that, always, it was *Jack*,
Not John.
Not disciple-like John, distinguished, inspired.
But plain, commonplace Jack.

Only other Jacks I knew as I grew were:
Jack Armstrong, Jack Armstrong, Jack Armstrong,
The All-American Boy on radio each day for Wheaties.
Knives called Jack that fit the leather sheath
Built on the shaft of my hightop knicker boots.
Oh, and Jolly Jack, my favorite candy bar till it defuncted,
And the Armstrong kid went off the air,
And I no longer wore boots
But still was Jack.

I wish I had been named Emmanuel.
That might have helped me define myself
Before I understood that I hadn't.
God with me I would have been reminded
Each time I spoke my name.

I didn't know that one of the most inspiring voices
In the rest of my patchwork life would be called by friends
Not C. S. Lewis but simply "Jack."

$10.00

This small book of poems was originally marked for sale
At nine-ninety-five.
Do you know what that was?
One might call it guile, clever salesmanship.
Apologizing, I acknowledge it as fraud.

Is a twenty-thousand dollar car too steep for you, friend?
Shall we say nineteen, nine ninety-five?

We've dropped the price of the house from a million-five
To only a mil-four ninety.

Do they think we don't know?

My father was an honest man.
He had a small station edge of town.
Called his gas *Pergas* ("Makes your engine purr")
In his prices were no decimal points.
If gas was selling for seventeen cents
He didn't say sixteen-point-nine.
"I don't think my patrons are fools," he told me once,
"So I don't try to fool them."

That, in so many ways, was a different time.

1898

C. S. Lewis was born in 1898.
My father was born in 1898.

Was Dad, I wonder and will never know,
Ever *surprised by joy*?
Did he find solace and a lift of life
In *Mere Christianity*?
He never told me.
My father in our living room never told me.
It took a stranger from abroad, through writings, even to begin
To reveal that which a son needs to know.
I'm glad that in addition to dad,
I also, through Lewis, met *Abba*.

Brother / Father

Why did I never have a chance
(Or make a chance)
To be a brother to my father?
Little enough was the time to be son.
Then he was off providing for all,
His weekends at home the slight time we had,
Moments to work on our HO layout
And that about all.
Then I was off to provision myself for what I had coming.

Was the failure mine?
I, too busy reaching for my sparkling new life-to-be
To note the diminishing sparkle of his?
Losing something, but too busy gaining, to care.
Now, time has passed and with it, he.
My own scintillations are subdued,
And I do not know, still do not know,
Was he proud of me? He never said.
Did he love me? It never showed.

I wonder, too, if he in his final days ever asked,
Was my son proud of me? He never said.
Did he love me? It never showed.

Augustine's Garden

While alone in the garden, a sudden sensation
Of peace descended and he was beguiled
By a butterfly of inspiration
Flitting on the voice of an unseen child.
The voice brought a curious message indeed,
One that seemed not directed at him
Yet he felt it a message he needed to heed,
That somehow that was expected of him.

Hedonist son of a pagan father,
Handsome of visage, hale, ruddy;
Excellent student when he would bother,
Excellent student — whom we still study
Thanks to that garden, that child's voice
"Take it up and read," it had said
And the hedonist fell on a life-changing choice
As he took up the Bible and in Romans he read:

The hour has come for you to wake up from your slumber
Because salvation is nearer now than we first believed.
The night is nearly over; the day is almost here;
So let us put aside the deeds of darkness
And put on the armor of light.
Let us behave decently, as in the daytime,
Not in orgies and drunkenness,
Not in sexual immorality and debauchery,
Not in dissension and jealousy.
Rather, clothe yourself with the Lord Jesus Christ
And do not think about how to gratify
The desires of the sinful nature.

Convicted, he left his life of sin
His concubine shed with no complaint;
The City of God he would live within
And the world would come to call him Saint

Friends:
When next in a garden, adore the flowers,
But listen and do not think it odd
Should you hear in those enchanted hours
An unseen child passing words from God.

America the Beautiful

Oh, how it hurts to sing that hymn
A favorite though it used to be
Enhanced by knowing how Katherine Bates,
In Colorado one summer to teach,
Rode an oxcart up Pike's Peak
And discovered . . . discovered . . .

From the top of that purple mountain majesty
She drank the fruited plain, the spacious skies,
Compounded those with back east recall of shining seas;
Then back at her hotel, took up pen
And quickly began to share her poetic dream
Of good all crowned with brotherhood,
Of God mending ev'ry flaw,
Of liberty confirmed in law.

Alas, however, we look today, we look away.
Her patriot dreams, her longing visions
Hard today to see.
Instead, where she found alabaster cities undimmed by human tears
We find rampant defalcations dimmed by human fears.
Our heroes today are too often proved
In unwise, futile strife.
We still wish that God might mend our ev'ry flaw
But in our courts we find not liberty
But licentiousness confirmed in law.
The only time we think seas shine
Is when we learn of a slick of oil.

I'm glad, Ms. Bates, you're not around
To see how your dreams fared.
They were worthy dreams and they still are;
The God you invoked has not let us down,
But we, I fear, are failing Him.
And you.

Being Transported

GPS setting the way,
Cruise control fixing the speed,
Satellite beaming music down;
I am being technologically propelled.
Transported.

Transported this moment by genius,
The genius first of a writer
Who memorably told of fated lovers,
And then by a tender composer
Who translated the tale to magical,
Uplifting, heart-pulsing music,
Capturing contentions 'tween families
Sublimely transcended by love, young love
— Wholly transporting!
Surely one of our greatest composers he was;
That's how we speak of Tchaikovsky today
Greatest composer, of him we say,
Not greatest *homosexual* composer.

Nor do we identify Copland as the gay creator of *Appalachian Spring,*
Nor Sondheim nor Porter as Queer Guys of Broadway.

Are those who wish *America the Beautiful*
Could be our national anthem
Not aware nor care that a lesbian wrote it?

I, for one, will stop what I'm doing
On hearing the haunted reverie of his *Adagio for Strings.*
But Samuel Barber, you tell me, was gay?

I say:
How transporting it will be when matters like that
We remember to forget.

Dumbness

Would that those across our land
Who persist in being so loudly dumb,

Were Zechariah dumb.

At This Moment

The first couple on earth sinned.
The first child born to the first couple murdered.
The Bible's great poet-philosopher-king
Had a man killed to take his wife.
This is the religion I follow?
The faith to which I pledge adherence?
There must be reasons, explanations, ways to understand.

At this moment, it is more important to me
To press my quest for those

Than write this poem . . .

Adult Adolescence

Psychologists speak of "Adult Adolescence."

As in —
Husband/father sharpens his wardrobe,
Touches up grey, buys a 'Vette,
Drives off to spread his seed in farther furrows.

As in —
Wife/mother feeling her own Itch
Whatever the year,
Abandons the patterned life she has
For the fancied life she has not
But is sure will give her freedom, let her grow.

He and she both assume that different will be better.
Both are adult.
Both, adolescent.
Both, as well, are wounders,
Leavers who knowingly damage the left,
Unknowingly, themselves as well.

Psychologists classify such as these,
And study them,
And dissertate upon them.

Which do no good at all.

Apotheosis

Why, so often, are we discontented
Wherever it is we happen to be?
Consider the comfort of woods surrounding,
Think of the creatures within them abounding,
Birds and animals we can't see
All invisibly represented.

Think of the hills, receding peaks,
Each a bit more vague than the last
As mist and distance push them away,
Away to where? Who can say?
Is it away into the past?
Or is it of future the far hill speaks?

And then beyond. The clouded beyond.
Clouds of promise, clouds to beware,
Clouds that reveal, clouds that secrete,
Clouds I feel I'd like to meet.
Clouds I think I would not dare;
All these, today, the sky has donned.

So this is something I wish I knew.
I often have this curious feeling
That someone — who, I do not know
Is carefully crafting these tableaux
To bring to my mind a bright revealing,
Apotheosis of all that's true.

Beep, Beep, Beep

The One! has power.
Power first flexed long ago
Power still, intrusive,
Invading, infecting, disturbing each one of our lives
Most every day.
Power is usually short-lived,
But not the enduring power unleashed by
The One!
Who was *The One?* that nameless person
Cubicled far away,
Unaccountable to you or me
Or to anyone accountable to us;
The dictater who years back dictated
Page after arcane page,
Feeling no doubt more personally powerful
Each paragraph, footnote, and codicil?
Who was it whose satanic scribbles
Would infringe even now
Upon my peace, my quietude?
How did that simple *One* of unsimple mind
Select the tone, the frequency precise:
One thousand hertz?
How designate the volume of emission:
97-112 decibels?
And interval: one strident second,
Most likely to command attention,
To torment and annoy?

Actually, we learn now that harping signal
Is not as effective at saving hard-hats
From rigs in reverse at construction sites
As it is at making those around, already safe,
Riled and dyspeptic.
Sometimes those we call civil servants are neither.

Bells

I hear bells in the distance, where they should be
Up close, bells tend to be sounding alarm
A break-in, a fire, someone done harm.
Someone at the door I don't want to see.

But hearing bells from a distance, we hear the real
Sonority a bell can bring;
And people smile and angels sing.
Of distant bells, peals appeal

Let them ring and peal and carry on
Their soothing sounds, their balm of aural ease
We need the sound of bells at distance please
That we might attend the angels' carillon

Choosing Icons

Two apps beckon as I take the chair
In my quiet place at start of day,
My place of retreating before I advance,
Of reflecting on other than self alone.
But first from my iPad those two symbols stare
Insistent that I look their way
Knowing that the way I first will glance,
That app will have me for its own.

The left one importuning so is *Mail*
Innocent enough now wouldn't you say
But once I click it I open the door
Not just to gossip and unfunny jokes
And hawkers touting their **Can't Be Beat Sale!
Don't Let This One Get Away**
And teases offering to sell me more
And pols and polls and arguing folks
Are those how I want to start my day?

The other icon is labeled *Prayer*
Insights of many wise women and men,
The Bible rendered in varied translation,
Commentaries to show the way
To follow the trail from here to there
And begin my gifted day again
Looking to God in jubilation,
Looking to God to start my day.

To which icon shall first I run?
Why so often do I choose the wrong one?

Civil?

See them.
They are not there, of course,
But see them as they were, when they were.
See the anguish of their living,
Fervent futility of their dying.

See them, ragged, bloodied, stumbling forth.
(The trees of the forest marching in more soldierly files than they
And hurting no one, nor themselves.)

Why did the men we cannot see yet know
Do as they did?
Any one of them could conjure a hundred hollow reasons
As he lay dying, musket-ball drilled clean through.
He might speak of slavery
The Right of Secession —
Men always have reasons for unreasonable acts.
Even lacking reasons,
They seem genetically driven to war,
Impelled to do whatever it takes
To get whatever they are persuaded they want.
Such incorrigible impulse denies,
The sanctity of the human soul.
But then I am here but as witness,
Visiting one of so many -- *too many* --
Warring grounds that bloodily ripped open
The bowels of our infant land a century-and-a-half ago.

The sensitive one of our family says
She can feel a pall,
A suffocating pall enshrouding the place.

The War Of Northern Aggression in some places known
By those who still fly Rebel flags.
(If *they* were rebelling how was the North aggressing?)
War Between The States is factual but mentions not the people.
Civil War, painfully contorts the language.
What, pray tell, was civil about it
Short of two gentlemen generals at its end?

Whatever called, the blood of then
Still pulses in the fevered blood of some today.
Re-creators, they call themselves,
Without explaining why such cataclysm
Wants re-creating.
Or, deeper, why they wish to do it.
Why do re-creators re-create what the Creator must have abhorred.
Is it that, unable to make their own wars,
They are left with re-making others?

For me, one tour through the pall of one appalling field
Satiates and sickens.

War should not be a spectator sport.

Cleansing Prayer

For me, it is kin to praying,
To hear the singing of Johnny Cash,
A smile-spreading, almost trembling thrill.
Not the prison songs,
Not Ring of Fire,
Gospel.

Elvis and the Jordanaires, offstage after shows, sang gospel
And, oh, how great they wert.
The Gaither band are peerless
But Johnny more than *singing* the Gospel,
Lived it.
In days of health and wealth,
In ending times of loss and painful authenticity
There he was considering "The Great Speckled Bird,"
Awaiting the inevitable meeting with "Dr. Death,"
Wishing only he could "Get my breath."
Till that time, he would sit forlornly but in faith
To hear the whistle of the "309."

Johnny and June together asking
Will the circle be unbroken?
Or pondering inevitability as one awaited the other
"On the Far Side Banks of Jordan."
That, the only song I know that still wells tears
And I every time unabashedly weep.
Such, for me, is cleansing prayer.

Lulu and the Lord

First thing the dear woman sees
As she wakens come early morn
Are loving eyes, the eyes of her much-adored dog
Snuggle-sandwiched there 'tween her and her husband,
Lulu, Lulu staring love.

Touched, as always, the woman closes her eyes again
And begins her day with this prayer:

> *Lord, help me to love you as perfectly,*
> *As purely and wholly*
> *As Lulu loves me.*

Creation Without Joy

Creation without joy is as lifeless
As life without creation is joyless.

I didn't write that line but wish I had.
It was in my book, a book I wrote,
So one might assume, and I am glad
To take credit for that thoughtful note

But I confess that those are lines
That were given me though it's hard to explain.
No tablets inscribed; no mystical signs;
No tricks or visions or legerdemain.

They simply appeared. iPad in hand,
I was writing a piece, knowing not
How to put the point I planned
To make. How to express the thought

Eluding me. Then here came those lines.
From where? I don't know. I could have refused
To accept them but he who so declines
Misses a God-offered chance to be used.

Cross of Shell

Painstakingly, with devotion and caring eye,
The artist starts to select from thousands of wishful shells,
Seashells collected by many hands over many years,
Now brought together, each hoping to be one chosen
To take its place as part of the homage to be created.

An observer harks back,
Imagining Borglum's sculptors blasting and chiseling
The granite of a Harney Black Hill,
Each node of rock hoping not to be stripped away
But may remain intact to be seen,
Perhaps as a facet of Lincoln's nose or TR's spectacles.
They all want to be part of the nation's new spectacle.

Is that how today thousands of seashells
Covering the artist's worktables feel?
They are not vying to be a president's nostril or glasses,
Nor tribute to monarch or tycoon, but rather a simple man
Miles and years away, known to us today by how he lived
And more vividly by how he died.
The artist creating the sign of the earthly end of a Creator,
Crafting a cross to be wholly sheathed in shells.

Eight foot tall it will be, and she knows not how to do it,
Has never dared adopt such a challenge.
All she knows which for her is enough
Is that somehow she will be guided.
In the night, in wakeful hours, will come visions, insights.
By morning she will know how to start the next part,
Deploying lightning whelk and olive shells to scallop edges,
Scallop shells to rhythmically adorn the face

In company with those, shells so aptly designated Angel Wings
On which she affixes the fossilized tooth of a megalodon shark
Vestige of millions of years past.
To encircle a sand dollar she crafts a doily of fighting conch.

Each day, new challenge; each night, new guidance.
Days and nights, month after month, taxing time, it will be
Before a creation to honor the Creator will be complete.
Then the burden and joy of hefting its fragility onto a pickup truck
Passing through curious traffic to reach the church,
And carefully, laboriously see it hoisted to its honored purple place.

There, this day, I gaze upon it with awe:
The symmetry, balanced by inspired asymmetry;
Rich variety bespeaking creation's abundance.
And the glow! The gleam!
I know the varnish she sprayed to enhance the shells,
Protect them. Still, for me the shine I see is the glow of God,
The gleam of His promises to us all.

Many will look upon the Cross with praise over days,
Some will look for the artist's name but find it not.
She demurred, insisting that she was never the artist,
Just privileged to serve for the nonce as The Artist's hands.

Curse of a Literal Mind

At times I feel cursed by a preter-literal mind.
No role has it when I'm walking the woods,
No place while strolling the banks of a stream.
A literal mind is not easily given to translate abstraction.
For it, words are tempered steel, thoughts inelastic.
"I say what I mean and mean what I say,"
I proudly, if tritely declare.
But what of the others?
What of the poets and writers of scripture
Who *say* what they *say* for they *mean* what they *mean*.

This bread is my body; Eat.
The wine is my blood; Drink.

When lilacs last in the dooryard bloom'd,
And the great star early droop'd in the western sky in the night

I struggle with those who do not shout dogma
But whisper allusive enigmas,
To me, those are shadows playing among the trees,
Ripples that weren't, but are and yet won't be.
Transcendent, abstruse.
My literal mind shudders and gags.
It needs recalibration,
A tune-up by the Greatest Enigma,
Re-birth into Ultimate Transcendence.

Dín

My life is din.
Has always been.
Din and clamor,
The hawking of hollows alleged to have glamor,
Mokes with mikes who do not know
Yelling at us who do not care.
Din.

To escape,
I must learn to grab life by the nape
And turn it around,
Must flee the sound,
The people-made noise,
That no one enjoys
Just uses to shield
From unrevealed
Discomforts of life,
Sameness or strife.
Noise will obscure,
They are sure, we are sure.
But no. It will not.

I must set myself free
Of rancid TV.

Do Not Know

I love it when singing brings us together by the river,
The beautiful, beautiful river
That flows, we sing, by the throne of God.

We are comforted when June assures Johnny
(With assurance we covet)
That when her time comes, then his,
She'll be waiting for him on the far side banks of Jordan

Is that how it is and will be
In death and after-life?
So we like to think, to sing,
To be re-united with those we love here on earth
We like to wish.
But we do not know. We do not know.
Is there really a river bestriding a throne
Upon which is seated Creator of All?
Did June await drawing pictures in the sand?
So we are told.
So we hope.
But we do not know. We do not know.
We are left with speculations,
Ours and predecessors',
Conjectural images drawn in the mind if not by it.
At one speculative time, it was art that arched a ceiling,
The artist, lying on his back,
Seeing God as an Ancient with flowing white beard.
That was his vision, his *tableau vivant*
It was not the Creator.

What does God look like?
Does he have an appearance
Discernible by our eyes and brain?
Our Book of Him says that we were created *In His Image*.
Does that mean, when my time comes to meet the great *I Am*
He will look like me?
I dread the thought but do not know.

And that I do not know is the only thing I know.

Do You Love Me?

You love me today; you tell me you do
Though I can't help but wonder:
Do you love me for what I am, as I am?
My body, each day more frail,
Random parts beginning to fail,
Hands tremble, arthritically ache,
Rising from a chair takes levering
My teeth sleep by the sink
I'm told a new knee will have to happen
That is how I am, and will be
Can you love that?

Or draw you still on a reservoir of memory,
Loving what I used to be? As I was?
I'll take that if that's how it is.
I'll take anything that keeps me living in your love.

Doubt

I doubt.
Not always, not *now*,
But on frequent *thens*.

Sometimes, trying to justify doubt, I wonder:
If I didn't doubt, would that mean I didn't believe?

Other times, still to justify, I wonder if Jesus doubted.
He had been, we are told, with the Creator since the Creation.
Nothing came into being without him, we're told.
But even accepting that,
Once he came to earth in human form,
Did he never feel human doubt?
Doubt of what he was, who he was?
As a human, did he ever forget he was anything more?

Do we, today, know what we are?
Are we human beings having spiritual experiences?
Or spiritual beings having human experiences?

Dove

Is it a symbol? Maybe a sign?
Or only what it seems, a bird?
Coincidence or Holy design
That I should see it while reading the Word?

It is during this morning's time of devotion
When there, out on the balcony
I notice something, a blur of motion
Through which I quickly come to see

On a terra cotta flower pot
That long has been deflowered, a bird
Alighted on its rim. Not
Announced, his stealthy arrival unheard.

He utters neither a call nor a coo
But still his very presence sings.
And what now do I see him do?
Of a sudden, he starts to flutter his wings

And rises softly in morning dim
(Still with not a whisper of sound)
Then settles. once more, back to the rim

But it's not a rim. I look around.
It's the shoulder of a man he is on
The robe on the shoulder of a man
What is happening here this dawn?
I hear a seraphic voice. Can

It be it speaks about the bird
As it intones *This is the one
With whom I am pleased.* That is His word
As I witness God blessing His son.

Dream-Deflaters

I am told I can't do it,
Be a fool to try.
It may be a dream I have harbored unspoken
For many and many of years.
But, no, I'm told, I should give it up.
You've got to be realistic.
Who do you think you are?

How poisonous, degrading, disabling
Such unsought denigration, denial can be.
Why would someone do that to someone?

Why would *I* do that to *me*?

Faith Alone

One needs more than faith in faith alone,
It is not enough to believe in believing.
To listen to prayer without yourself praying
Makes it a self-serving, circular exercise,
God excluded.

Faith must be rooted in someone to be your own
Companion, at your side, never leaving
You to be alone, always staying
With you, making your life a golden prize,
God included.

Fire

Salute
Salute

The compelling power of fire for good or ill,
Lambent tongues of rampant flame
Uncontrolled, they ravage, destroy.
Controlled, clear deadfall and brush,
Making healthy the woods.

Fire, destroyer,
Fire, friend
Fire, the sun
Warming, lighting, fueling our lives.

Fire, the core of our planet
Randomly bursting forth in pyrotechnic display
Fire, *our* core too,
The fire of our being, lit within us by God
Residing, ever, eternal,
The Spirit igniting our thoughts, our ways, our essence.

Salute
Salute

Four Friends

One friend's wife deserted him and their four kids.
One friend's memory dissolved, his balance grew un-.
One friend's chemo started again though now with little hope.
One friend suffered heart attack, stroke, now therapy thrice.

It's tough having friends at this stage of life;
It's good having life at this stage of friends.

Friend

But still I ask:
Have I ever had a friend?
For that, have I ever *been* a friend?
Not a chum, not a hang-around bud,
Telling jokes, going to games. Not that alone,
But a full-fellowship friend,
Intimately sharing everything — everything
In my heart, my mind, my life,
Both secrets and shames,
Matters I don't even speak of to God.
Could I ever do that with a person, a friend?

It would be like unzipping my skin,
Taking it off,
Exposing heart and lungs,
Seeing where the prostate used to be
And where the one remaining kidney is;
I could have a scan done of my brain
But that wouldn't scan my mind
So what would be accomplished?
Would it bind even closer friend to friend?
Could I or friend ever do it?
Create that sort of friend the Apostle John spoke of where
You are in me and I am in you.
That is a friend worth seeking.

Genealogy

In December of sixteen-hundred-ten
By the Gregorian now employed,
Something happened to change my life.
Something and many more somethings would have to happen
Not merely to change my life but make it be at all.

On that ancient December day in Hamptonshire, England
A young woman named Patience
Espoused a young man named Edward,
Edward Perkins.
For me that was thirteen generations back.
Thirteen cycles of women and men who happened to meet
Came to love, chose to wed, gave birth to sons and daughters
Who in their turn would come upon just the right mates
To produce the right offspring
To keep the golden chain of miracle unbroken,
Inviolable, link after link.

But think:

One meeting centuries back of fated lovers unfulfilled,
One courting appointment disregarded,
One childbirth gone awry, one baby lost,
One youngster felled by fever sweeping the town,
One hurrying carriage crushed by falling tree,
    Town doctor never to reach a fevered child;
One man found impotent; one wife, barren;
One husband, disenchanted, leaving home;
One marital spat precluding one coupling one night;
One warrior slain in futile war;
One girl's family failing to move to the colonies;
One boy's emigrating kin choosing a different locale . . .

All of the links
The *almost weren'ts*
The *might-have-been's*
In any single one of those
For all those miles,
All those years, all those centuries,
Plus all the other times and connections before my ken,
Had there been but a single interruption,
A single snap of a single link of that golden chain,
Today there would be no *me*.

I want to express my gratitude
Though somehow it doesn't seem right to say:
"Thank you, Coincidences."

Glimmer

At first it is a glimmer of glow on the water,
Spread on the smooth of the water before me.
The world around is humble silhouette
Awaiting the glimmer to grow.
(The world around knows its place; Do I?
Does the glimmer come to remind me?)
As I watch, the glow appears no longer spread *on* the water
But somehow imbued *within* it, rising from it,
The sea its seeming source;
And it grows more luminous and throbbing.

What can it be *in* or *of* the sea to pulse such holy light?
Light in which devotedly I bathe,
A soothing morning ablation albeit too short-lived
For the glow the sea was emitting begins to dim,
So at first it seems. But, no.
It only seems to dim because slowly it is being outshone.
Now comes truth:
That glimmer of glow at the start was not subaqueous,
Neither *in* nor *of* the water,
But only reflected, serving as merely a preview, a tease.
For here comes the show. Here, the star.
A sliver at first, peeking through silhouettes,
Scoping things out.
Burning intensely through tree-forms as through a mountainside bush,
A burning bush, flames unquenchable.
I dare not approach it.

The sea at this revealing moment is Holy ground
Aflame ever brighter, greater and higher
Till the sky itself explodes in color,
Colors dancing to celebrate
The star that is the sun,
The Son who is of the Father.
Rising.

If I do not worship at this moment
In this place,
I should not be permitted to worship
Anywhere, anytime, anymore,
Ever.

God of Fog

God of fog,
In mist are your mysteries enshrouded,
Even as I am oft befogged myself.

Golden Nuptials

Half a century ago,
We stood, that God-given girl and I
In a small town Ohio church
Sprung from Dutch tradition,
Stood to hear the incantation
That would bind us two as one.

Now, on this Golden Remembrance Day,
We God-blended two
Are drawn to an unknown church by its beckoning bell
Pealing across a warm-wind island miles from our home.
A great rock structure, it is,
Three story vaulted ceiling
Ornate chandeliers swaying in breezes above us
As we stiffly sit in rock-hewn pews on stone floor
Gazing up at the ship-prow pulpit where
One after another men and women, ceremonially garbed,
Proclaim their faith, God's promise
In words we do not know though their meanings we do
All prayers, hymns, readings, sermon rendered in Dutch
In this church still adhering to Dutch tradition
As it has for two-hundred-forty years
On this Dutch bred island far from its Ohio echo.

The language we cannot hope to understand
Nor need we.
The Spirit understands the words being spoken and sung
And we the Spirit know.

It is our interpreter
Rehearsing our golden nuptials
More vividly than language ever could.

For important times like this, words would get in the way.

Greeks

More and ever more are we become a land of Greeks.
Not Greeks of now but Biblical Greeks --
Intelligent, even slaves to their intelligence.
Proud of their knowing without always knowing
What lay beyond knowing.

As they were, often are we:
Gentile philosophers of barren pragmatism.
Do not ask us to believe that an executed criminal,
A dishonored small town carpenter millennia past
Has any bearing on us. We are not fools;
We do not accede to foolishness.
We welcome the profusion of books of late that defy and deny
What churchly folk are taught and try to teach us,
Books that seek to dispel the phantasms of a god above us,
Above all.
Books that bring us back to the ancient Greekness
That once bedeviled the great Apostle himself.

Between then and now, have been backsliding times
As when those who would establish a nation
Found themselves earnestly proclaiming
That God was the author and enabler of their dreams
And some of their insightful successors would proclaim the same
But, as time passed, proclaim with less and less conviction,
So it seemed.
Till one day one leader baldly, boldly said
Ours was not a Christian nation anymore.
He might as well have told us plain:
We, at last, again, are ancient Greeks.

Greens

Billowing land beneath the wing:
America the ripe,
America the green.
No, not just green but
Green and green and green; multitudinous,
The verdure of the billow-pillow hills below.

Set me down; put me in those woods
Awaking on a summer morning
Certain I can see at least twenty-three
(Or twenty-three hundred)
Greens that weren't here before
Let me survey, absorb and give thanks
To a provident God who arranged that my eyes
Can distinguish more greens than any other hue
More than a million did someone say there are?
I believe they all surround me here in these woods today.

Fred

I didn't want to make the call;
I dreaded having to make the call;
I *had* to make the call.

Over times, so many of the best had been with him.
Working, playing, cavorting 'round much of the world
On deadline assignments . . . with him.
Broadcasting live a solar eclipse
From the deep of a Mexican jungle?
Never been done before. We did it, he and I.
Wars in the East, wars to the South,
And, always, politics, which we hastened to forget,
He and I.
He and I and our wives and kids
Made gluttons by Fred-Burgers
Fourth of July at their place;
Treasure-hunted eggs in the lawns at our place
Easter morning. Finding eggs but knowing that they were not
The true treasure of the day.
Raiders' games, Hollywood Bowl, birthdays,
Most any celebration shared with them.
With him.

Through all, he and I respected each other so much
We would never think of admitting we loved each other too.
Men don't. Men don't do that until . . .

Was it too late as our phone call came to an end and I finally
Extended that tardy confession?
I love you, Fred.
His weakened voice seemed to muster a bit of strength:

Thanks, Jack. Thank you.
For the call? For the years? For the love?
As I hung up the phone, I wondered:
If Fred was the one dying,
Why was I the one crying?
Was it perhaps for myself,
Funereal tears, mourning not the deceased
But the weeper's personal loss?
Shouldn't a believer joyfully celebrate
A fellow believer's passing to God's presence?

Were my tears, then, not only for what I was losing,
But, as well, for fear?
Fred was a few years my elder.
Two years back, fit and seemingly healthy,
He had no concern for strokes or cancerous bladder,
Thought not of those.
I, today, think not of such.
Will some old friend of mine a couple years hence
Be dreading having to make *that call* to me?

Requiem

He stumbled on steps from restaurant to street
His wife and mine, ahead, did not see
As the small man wearing the large black coat
Wearing, also, eighty-six years,
The trembles of Parkinson's, memory of stroke
And the ghost of Guillan-Barré, dropped to the steps.
I reached out my hand to help him up
But he laughed, "Good thing about being short;
You don't have as far to fall."
That was the only unoriginal thing I ever heard Fred Craddock say.

Before I was blessed to meet and befriend him,
I knew him.
Small-town preacher, big-city teacher of preachers,
He, his speaking and writing, it was said, shaped the American church.
Country preacher become country's preacher.

After his laugh-it-off stumble that day
Fate had it arranged I would not see him again
Short days later came the word:
Another fall, this his final, felled him at home
He had worked in his study,
The teacher still learning, the writer composing,
Then retired to bedroom to nap.
It was then, it was there, that came his ultimate call.
He knew. He must have known
Rising from bed he headed not for help
But toward the door
As though to respond, always faithful, to the call.
This time when his wife heard the fall she understood;
She knew.
Rescuers came but, as he could have told them, could not rescue.
Savers cannot save whom the Savior has called.

Cuz

This is a story I told my fellowship friends:

Hey, guys, up in Georgia last week
I had a nice chat with my cousin one day
Not enough chances do I have to be with him,
My only cousin, only recently found.
As kids we never met each other
(His dad and mine weren't friends, we surmise)
Yet when, in mid-life, we finally met, Cuz and I,
Against odds, we instantly liked, soon respected
And came to love each other,
To treasure our precious cousin-ness

So here I was now visiting him in his room
Bringing his favorite candy; that yielded a smile
(Reese's does that too to me)
We set to mellow reminiscing, though mostly one-way
I talked of the company he used to head
How everyone there misses him so
They insisted I pass on their greetings;
Must be engaging memories there, huh?
Talked of our wives; we're both greatly blessed,
Talked of the trip he took to the hills for a grandson's wedding
Can Casey really be that old! Don't you remember when ...
He didn't.
Didn't remember that or much else
It was a challenging chat that day with Cuz.
I wish he had been there.

As I finished my story, my fellowship friends
Posed one question:
Do you think the frustration you felt
When you couldn't get through to your Cuz --
                      Is what God too often feels with us?

Obit for Norm

Hold (A Long Time, I Hope) for Release

He never seemed a holy man,
Nor cast himself in such a role.
He was small town through his span
Of years; small town in his soul.

Lobsterman, lawyer, tiller of soil,
Head of a savings and loan was he.
Not one to shrink from honest toil,
Nor toil without honesty.

"I'll never be rich," he told a friend
"But no one can claim I wasn't just"
As he spread hanks of seaweed from end to end
Across our asparagus patch whose crust

He had rototilled the day before,
Not doing it because he's just,
But just because. Is there more
To ask than his kind of kindness and trust?

That may not make him a holy man
But the consistent course of his life surely did.
I say "Did" because the race he ran
Would run down at last and he never hid

From reality, from finality.
He had a good life but had read the text;
He accepted with grace his mortality
Because he knew what was coming next.

Graves

Don't put me in the ground,
In a box in the ground,
Flowers adorning, (plastic saving water).
Do not bury me.
(Though of course the request is vaporous;
For there shall be no "I" to box.)
The "I" of me will have — What?
Disappeared? Fled? Been transported to unseen realm?
I do not know the answer to that and that, for me,
Is the answer.

When the body I have worn these many years
Wears out,
Think of it no longer as me.
No need ponder what to do with it.
It is only "It."
Plant it in the ground?
Might it, moldering, nourish lively, non-plastic flowers?
Then, fine.
Otherwise, let it go, pay no heed.
Disregard the "It"
The "I" of me, though, please keep close to you
As long as there remains a *You* of you.

Life

I hesitate to say it,
Reluctant, even in the seclusion of these pages,
To plunge into such roiled waters,
Become embroiled in such broiling scorch
Of controversy lurking.
I have always avoided speaking out.
But now, I am told — and am sold —
I must.

Not a meet matter for disquisitions,
Convincing answers aren't found in unbrief briefs
Or judicial pronouncements.
They are not the scat of jurisprudence
But the child of one's deep-heart conviction.

Those who presume to count such things tell us
That most in our nation today believe in God.
Let that majority, then, look to the words of that God,
Look, read, and understand.
It is not hard. The words are plain, meanings clear.

Till now, I have dodged and diverted
Whenever the subject came into view.
Why should I say what I feel and maybe upset folks?
Now I understand:
I should upset folks in order to set folks up.
Set them up to openness instead of tired shibboleth.
Phrases that if they ever had meaning it has eroded away

Pro Choice --
Wasn't the phrase forged to make an awful evil
Seem somehow harmless? Banal?
More honest slogan would have been:
Pro-Killing-Babies-Not-Yet-Born.
Choice sounds so much better.

Wish people would be honest,
Encourage thinking rather than selfish, rote regurgitation.

Birthday Talk with God

God, give me the strength to carry on
With the work you would have me do. I'm getting old;
My muscles are weakened, energy too soon gone.
So much to do, so little vigor ...

    Hold!

A voice. Loud though silent yet clearly heard
Chastising, taking me to task
For my every self-pitying, whimpering, whiny word.

> *Young One who thinks himself old, how dare you ask*
> *For what I have already given; I granted you vigor*
> *And what have you done? Squandered it most away.*

Well, I have a treadmill, have a bike, I figure
I could use them more but it seems that every day . . .

> *... You get so busy you can't take care of the gift*
> *I have given, your body, my Temple.*

But, God, I try.

> *A try, my son, is a failure. You cannot lift*
> *Yourself by merely trying. You must apply*
> *Yourself and do! Change anticipated*
> *Isn't change until it's finally been completed.*
> *Only then will those corrugated*
> *Abs be no longer just folds of sagging skin.*

People ask if I am unwell. I'll
Hear them say "You're looking awfully drawn."

> *Then, do you know what to do? It's simple. Smile.*
> *With a smile on your face, drawn is gone.*

I've a bad right knee, cartilage shot

> *And I provide doctors to care for such.*

Left hand, a tremor.

> *You write with your right, that's not*
> *A problem.*

Been losing weight, I don't think too much.

> *Sign of discipline or of decline?*
> *Losing fat is good, but you are losing*
> *Muscle. In aging, not a healthy sign.*

But, Lord, understand, that is not my choosing
I've had three cancers; one kidney remains . . .

> *Stop complaining. I've told you you need only one.*
> *Now listen, child, as your God explains:*
> *All I could ever do for you I've done.*
> *From here on, more of that "all" will be up to you.*

Up to me to make my life anew?

> *With my guidance.*

And if I make it as you say?

> *Then call this your Happy Re-birth Day.*

Horrid Hyphen

So there hangs that horrid hyphen,
Dangling, denoting my incompletion.
Let us call it not a dash.
Dash would make it sound too eager
To close the circle, tally the sheet,
Beginning-end, Alpha-Omega,
Append those final digits
That I am not eager to know.
1933 —
How unbalanced the equation remains
Simply because stubbornly, I have not yet demised.
Give me, please, more time.
Let the horrid hyphen hang,
Dangling, denied its terminal digits for yet a long, long while.

Having The Dream

Sometimes the headline is better than the story;
Anticipation glows brightly; reality dims.
Anyone dreaming of loving and being loved
Should understand the odds: accept that
Sometimes *In love* is all there's going to be.
Not all dreams come true;
It may be enough just to have the dream.

Ignorance

Like waves rolling on sandy beach;
Like scurrying birds dashing away, dashing back
To keep from being sluiced away;
Like manta rays, their shadows sliding ghosts offshore;

Like everything I can see or imagine I can see,
Like all of these, each one,
I am ignorant.

They don't know it.
It would mean nothing to them if they did.
But I know I don't know and it makes a difference.
It shames and ought to humble me.
For I, unlike the waves and birds,
The rays and clouds and fish to sea,
Know better.
My ignorance, you see, is not want of knowing
But caring.
Uncaring, I ignore.
Too much that I should be attending,
For convenience or for ease
I ignore.

Hummingbird

I don't deserve my prayers to be heard;
I shouldn't really call them prayers.
I go to my secret place at dawn,
Close my eyes with intent to pray
But interrupting thoughts steal prayer away.
My good intendings quickly gone,
My fractious mind flitting from *here's* to *there's*
Like a hyperkinetic hummingbird.

I figure it happens this way because
My mind is so stuffed with stuff folks are saying
On radio, TV, everywhere,
About the crime and perilous time.
It makes me all the more certain that I'm
More than ever in need of prayer.

This poem came when I should have been praying.
Maybe I was, maybe I was.

Indelicate?

Maybe it wasn't the best way to put it. Okay.
Not the most seemly, saying nothing of thoughtful.
After fifty-five years, though, she knows
I am not always seemly or thoughtful.

We are waiting a takeoff for which our habit long has been
Clasping hands.
(At times, even flying alone, I find myself reaching out
To her hand, imagined.
Simply the gesture comforts.)
This time, together, we join our hands,
Hers over mine over hers.
And, as always, I feel so tingly alive and in love
As I survey the topography of hands:
The intricate gnarls and knobs,
("Arthur" at work.)
Skin like crepe paper,
Translucent, mapping the pale blue byways of aging blood,
Tendons, muscles, and everywhere those telling sags of skin

I blurt:

Dear, I think it is God's greatest gift to me
That I have been permitted to be here all these years,
Wrinkling with you.

Is It Enough?

Is writing poetry enough?
Does scribbling occasional verses fulfill
The obligation I am assigned
To comfort the hurting, offer light
In the darkness, evil rebuff
Can I be expected still
To nourish soul, strengthen mind
While all as a poet I do is write?

When I make photos of beautiful scenes
Re-envisioning God's creation
I am a copyist, that is all
My photo's not beauty; the subject is
I'm grateful for compliments, by all means
I vainly accept my share of ovation
But I wish well-wishers would try to recall
They celebrate not my work but His.

Junk File

Alas, we did not plan this,
Did not intend or desire this,
But somehow, defying our wishes
Transcending our thoughts,
It happened. Is happening.
Rue to us all.

Our world, without our desiring,
Has become a password world.
Passwords, PIN's, and codes to remember,
Or forget. Mostly forget.

Want to pump gas? What's your PIN?
Collect your email? Password, please.
Forget your password? User Name?
Oh, yes, you need that too.

We are become -- Damn the spots! -- high-tech.
What? You did not want to be high-tech?
Sorry, there was no opt-out option
On the electronic form you must have received in your email.
Didn't you?
Check. It might have gone to your Junk file.
Know how to access that? You should.
That's where most of our lives are going.

Let Me Wallow

How many birds are living
In the waters and air of earth?
How many species,
How many colors?
No, don't Google,
I prefer simply to ponder;
Not solve a mathematical equation,
Not census or index,
Just let me reflectively,
Lovingly,
Gratefully
Wallow in wonder.

Margins

Off to the margins of my life
I push problems I don't wish to address,
There they are exiled,
Off where the people I choose to ignore,
Most often pass by, ignoring,
For they, too, are dispatched to the margins.
The things I need to do,
The things I should have done
I push them there.
All that, I guess, is human nature,
And so, I'm afraid, is this:

Most of the time, out to the margins
I push God.
Putting him there to wait till I need Him.
Unconscionably arrogant, human nature.
But not uncommon.
What an exhilarating feeling
To know that I can control God
Put him wherever I want Him,
Whenever,
And can bring Him back from the margins
Just when I need Him.
I feel like God's god.
I, in the center: never the margins.

Mary/Martha

Martha, sometimes Mary am I,
Asunder within myself.
Jesus comes to my home, comes every day
That by Him I might be guided on the way.
And I sit at His feet. the Mary of me, eager to learn.
While my Martha putters with matters more urgent--
Checking weather,
Reading mail,
Puttering about the kitchen of life, the Martha of me.
She knows that Mary is well advised and strangely
Resents that she herself is not at His feet.
She should be; I should be.
How many mornings have I still the chance?
Yet my Martha too often prevails.

Mean Wishes

How often have you wished
(Truth, now!)
Wished unkindly, meanly perhaps,
But fervently,
That all who design those "Easy Open" packages
Be sentenced to spend Eternity
Trying to open them.

Mirror

The mirror is old,
"Antique," said the shop. Shops do.
No question, though, it has known many faces,
Before being faced now with mine.
My face wrinkles and twists in its wavering glass
As though reflected on the sossling waters of a murky pond,
Or thrown back at me from a funhouse glass.
Clots of floating debris speckle my face,
The back of the mirror spottily desilvered.
Rendering but a teasing puzzle of me,
A being not yet fully assembled.

Maybe it's right.

Morning Prayers

Day's first rays my cue to go
To my private morning place of prayer
Secluded room, welcoming chair
Only light the electronic glow

Of an iPad displaying others' prayers;
What Warren and Yancey have to say,
Lewis and Chambers from back in their day,
Spurgeon, Augustine —love to read theirs.

Daily words of devotional writing,
Recorded churchly music and thought,
So many lessons being taught.
So much Holy Spirit igniting

That, rising from my morning chair
I feel sanctimonious I dare say.
Fulfilled and ready for the day.
Just one thing: In that time of prayer,
I never did take time to pray.

Morning Star

And a star fell into the water,
A morning star, the sun.
Am I the only one who thinks it odd to find
The sunken sun still shining brightly in the water,
Still a beacon to those around?
But for how long? The overhanging tree
Points a drooping branch with incredulity
At what must, for it, be a damning sight:
Its life-force drowned.

Worry not, wary tree;
Worry not, son and daughter;
Be assured: the Holy Light
Cannot be drowned in dark unholy water.
One of doubting mind is urged
To see this as analogy
(That and nothing more),
A way for us to realize
That what may seem today submerged
Lost and buried may once more rise.

It happened before.

My Hymn

The song I would write,
Were I composing a hymn to creation,
Would begin with a tremolo hummed by bass clarinets,
Perhaps a grunting bassoon, woody and soft.
Joined in sixteen bars by flutes in lower register,
Harmony throbbing gently.
The melody picked up by the voice of a hermit thrush,
Wings in the wings, unseen.
And for the chorus:
Tree frogs, cicadas, cooing doves, punctuating crows,
All their voices underlain by breeze through unbarbered trees,
And for rhythm, the flapping of a thousand wings,
Eider on the sea below,
Surf, it's pounding compounding paradiddles on granite shore.
The crescendo builds and a spotlight of sun sets fire,
Exploding earth and sky to reveal what lies beyond.
Humbled, I stand mute.

There are no lyrics to my hymn,
None composed, none required.
Ask Debussy, Copland, Williams:
There's no need for words when the music is right.

My Way

Was I born that way?
Brought up that way?
Can I never break away from that way?

Methodical, mechanical engineer, my dad.
Debate, my chosen school time sport.
Syllogistic logic, favorite college course.
Journalism, fall-into career,
Sealing my fealty to fact, provable fact
In lieu of unfounded speculation.
Those were my way,
Those were always my way as though ordained
By a Power not ordinary.

How now to move from my long ways to His?
From deifying the known and defying the un-
To seeing what cannot be seen.
Letting not truth but Truth be my guide,
Trusting in that which I cannot prove,
What surely is not syllogistically logical,
And I no longer am prone to debate
As from fact to faith my way matures.

Naming Things

Why do so many want their names on things?
Exchanging wealth for recognition.
I give you five mil;
That dorm, evermore, trumpets me.
Deal!

Can charity be real if conditional?
Should *quid pro quo* benevolence be praised?
Is the compensated giver really giving?

The politician or his heirs
Don't have to let the graceful span across the bay
Be named for him.
Wasn't "Sunshine Skyway" felicitous
Without prefixing an old pol's name?
Sure, he had something to do with its doing.
But . . . .

My grandfather and his brothers, more than a century back,
Erected an interstate bridge that still spans the Delaware River,
Independent, faithfully serving the people about.
And it is not named The Perkins Bridge.

I thought this all had been fairly resolved
Back in Matthew Six.

Nebo

I rise above the plains of Moab
Climb to the top of my own private Nebo;
Gaze from the mount to see for myself the Promised Land.
Earnestly I peer through eyes of given faith,
But I see not so much a Promised Land
As a promised way to live;
Henceforth, the voice of a Spirit speaks to assure
That when I trek harsh mountain tracks,
Or wander peaceful valley paths
Though I be by myself . . . I shall not be alone.

Nevermore alone: That is the promise of Nebo to me.
Not what I expected . . . more than I deserve.

Pile Driving

Oh, but the builder was proud.
Proud of the overwrought island house
He had finally completed
After many months of toil and turmoil.
One month alone given solely to pounding.
Ninety concrete pilings each thirty and something feet long
Had to be driven into island rock and soil
By a savage beast machine, it's powerful sledge
Driving a piling just one quarter inch
For each brutal, earth-shaking pound.
Meaning there had to be pound after pound after pound after pound
After pound after pound after pound after pound after pound —
A relentless barrage of piles driven
While homes adjacent shook and cracked as did the people inside.
Ah, but in the end how the builder was proud!
Hurricane could come and wash this whole island away, he told me with pride,
But this house will still be here.

My question:
Why?

Prayer

If, when praying, we raise our eyes to skies,
We do so to acknowledge the infinitude of God.

If, rather, we close our eyes and bow,
We warrant as well His indwelling

There is no proper way to pray
Or place or time.
As long as it is everywhere and always.

Quibbles

Some churchgoers wave their hands when singing hymns;
Some complain of those who wave their hands when singing hymns;
Some fret that the hymns are always the same-old, same-old;
Some disdain the ones they've never heard before.
Some enjoy repeating lines over and over;
Some think it puerile, not fit for their Deity.

They are quibbling people who make such complaints.
I have heard none from God.

S. D. G.

Three naked letters inscribed on a musical score,
Marking a great man's humility.
On hundreds of pages of genius, then hundreds more,
Did he pen those letters: S. D. G.

In his life of composing Bach was little renowned,
But that inscription was witness he need not care,
He composed not that fame for himself be found.
But that the glory should be placed where

It truly belonged: S. D. G.
Soli Deo Gloria.
"To God alone let all the glory be"
To God, the giver of holy euphoria.

Handel chose to inscribe Messiah the same.
Disdaining praise for self so all who would hear it
Would know forever he was only the name
On a score composed by the Holy Spirit.

As in more recent days of popular song,
A wedding song set down by a believer,
Noel Paul Stookey, who all along
Knew he was not the composer, but the receiver

Of a sanctified preachment Bible-born and inspired.
His role: messenger to those who knew
Of Peter, Paul and Mary and as they admired
Their work they heard the Word and remembered it too:

A man shall leave his mother and a woman leave her home
And they shall travel on to where the two shall be as one.
As it was in the beginning is now and till the end
Woman draws her life from man and gives it back again.
And there is love. there is love.

Oh the marriage of your spirits here has caused him to remain
For whenever two or more of you are gathered in his name,
There is love, there is love.

S. D. G.

Corwin

Would that we still had a Corwin today,
A Norman Corwin, as of old;
And also an outlet for his art.
A place that would understand his place.

He was the poet laureate of a medium
That today no longer feels a need for poetry.
Radio docudramas, I guess they'd be called today,
But there seems no appetite for them anyway.
And no Corwin to create them.
Losing him was loss indeed.

He mined the rich veins of our being,
Knew the pains and fears that haunted;
Knew, too, and could voice our greatness
Just when we were doubting ourselves.

He set us all to a score that needed no music
Save for that of his silvery phrases,
Mellisonant words.

He paid tribute,
Laid a poultice upon our national sores.
He inspired or incited whichever was needed.
He knew us better than we knew ourselves
But from his knowing and telling, we learned.

A war ending, a war needing fought,
Sacrifices made, honor given, spirits buoyed?
Call Corwin.
He will inscribe upon the ether,
Dispatch across the radio waves,
A nation's heart, a people's soul
And we all will be better for it.

Ah, but no more. Radio moved on.
Not improved, moved on.
It has no room for a Corwin today,
Though we need him more than ever.

Ripple

One ripple, just one in a rapidly rippling stream.
I fix in my gaze as I sit on the grassy bank
Watching the shiny patterns of that single ripple,
Tumbling rolls of water on water
Cavorting among the sparkling bubbles playing chase
The ripple, ever changing yet unchanging
New water supplanting old but dancing the same aquatic ballet
In quite the same places.
The scene, constantly moving
And movingly constant

I know not what lies beneath the waters to incite the dance.
The stream is shallow and clear.
I could tell if I wished
But I do not wish;
To discover the cause of something of beauty
Too often demeans and dispels it

Ah, would that I were a ripple,
Tumbling and shining and laughing,
Blessing all who look upon me
As well as those at distance who only hear my bubbling glee.

Same Time, Next Year

We do it each year; have for twenty-five
Same time, same place,
Harraseeket country inn, Freeport, Maine
Fresh as approaching Christmas,
Familiar as warming memories.
Rest of the year we may not see our friends,
Unlikely hear from them
But they are old friends, dear friends,
Even not when near friends.
A person is accorded few of those in life;
They are neither to be squandered or neglected.
So we honor this annual time of catching up.

— Took the whole family, kids and grands, to the Galapagos.
— Young ones must've loved that.
— All did. Got pictures on the iPad. How 'bout you?
— My travels were mostly plugging the book. Heartwarming response
— And Jo?
— I am so proud of her. Tell 'em, Jo.

We don't talk politics; we differ there
And this is not the time for differences.
We don't talk religion. It seems more realized in us than them.
We talk of past and future.
Oh, and, yes, we eat.
Proudly the Inn lists its local purveyors,
And its chefs do proud their wares.

There is that.
But mostly, our time on these fond gatherings each year is spent

A few blocks down the way, down to the heart of the little town,
Where Leon Leonwood Bean founded a little store years before.
It has grown, amoeba-like since then
As has its town, spangled now with all sorts of shops
Offering all the things that people need.
Need?
Where is the line between *Need* and *Want?*
We test that enigma, the four of us, day after wearying day.

One of us finding that his favorite shoes aren't made anymore
Buys up the last four pair his size.
Need?

Sending Prayers

All too often we hear people say
I'll be praying for you.
They won't.
God knows there are many more pledges of prayer
Than prayers.

We hear the glib pretend-believer proclaim on TV,
Our prayers certainly go out to the family.
Sorry, Posing Proclaimer, that's not
The right place to go them out.

Singing Hymns

How many of us just mouth the words?
Or, singing gustily, profane by our insincerity?
How many sing the words *out*
But fail to sing them *in.*
Maybe our words will help others, we think,
While not letting them help ourselves.

Did hymns help Elvis?
After performing to smoke and sin,
After onstage adulation,
Did he gather with friends in shadow hours
To sing gospel together as antidote?
Assured by faces and cheers how great he was,
Did he need reminding Who really is?
(Do we all need reminding?
Continuous, convicted reminding?)
Did Elvis, in his final murky hours of pills and despondency,
Fatally find that after all his years of singing *out* his faith

> *Take your troubles to the Chapel,*
> *Get down on your knees and pray;*
> *Then your burdens will be lighter*
> *And you'll surely find your way.*

                                              He had failed to sing it *in.*

Or what of Randy.
His dulcet cello voice telling how love lifted him,
But telling not what demons brought him down
To wandering streets, naked and bleeding.
The lyrics he left us,
Are we intended still to believe them?
Does he?

Do I, upon writing these verses,
Verses I think of as poems of praise,
Read them, ingest them, absorb them, believe them?
Or only write them?

Come Sit with Me at Sunrise

I once wrote a poem:
Come Sit With Me at Sunset
About our lives, the two of us,
About our one-day deaths, the two of us,
About our always, now and then
Being blessed to be together.

In the partnering photograph three chairs stood;
I was several times asked, "Is the third one for Jesus?"
Engaging thought (that had not been mine)
In the view I see now are only two chairs
(Jesus now indwelling?)
And it pictures the rise not the setting of sun.
Hence:

Come sit me at sunrise.
One more sunrise given us;
They grow more precious do they not?
Each an Alleluia, some a challenge, some a test
But always Alleluia!

What will this new day offer us?
What will it demand?
I'm glad we don't know.
If we knew, how trite would be life
In routine we do not grow.
And regardless the calendar
We still are creatures created to grow,
Grow in ourselves, of ourselves, though never by ourselves;
He of the unseen chair is always with.

Let us then accept this floridly forthcoming day
Inspired by the beauty of the sunrise.
Let us make the day it heralds even better,
You and I.

And Him.

Skaters

Two branches of family,
Normally distance-divided,
Come together to honor the day of the Patriarch's birth.
After so long apart there is much to say, to share
About health and well-being,
Hobbies, travels and work,
Problems and prides.
There's much to ask and much to answer,
Much to learn and share.

Instead, a curtain descends.
A shroud of personal privilege
Announcing, unspoken, that
If you don't ask, I won't have to duck an answer.
We'll all be better off.

On the table, grandly set for Birthday Feast,
The centerpiece is one of those mirror ponds
Across which glide carefree plastic skaters,
Crissing this way, crossing that,
Always skating the surface,
Reflecting only themselves in their playful cavortings,
Nothing deeper, nothing beyond,
But they're happy,
Very happy.
So very surface happy . . .

So All Shall Know
(Especially me)

Let me put it down.
Make it indelible, ineradicable,
Boldface, italics and underlined.

I know the time may come my memory curdles
(Sadly, I saw it in a friend.)
What now I know I may not then.
Synapses snapped.
So let me put it down while still I can:

That beautiful , blessed spirit at my side is my wife!

Sounds

Sounds abound around but I shall only hear them if I try.
I must aurally focus upon them to know them.
They are not like noises which, too, abound,
Those are people-induced and insistent;
I have to make effort *not* to hear those,
Aurally unfocus to melt them away
That I might in their stead hear *sounds*
Nature-made.
God-given.

On Seeing a Sun Halo

How did it come to look like this?
The afternoon Florida sun
Ringed with shadow and halation;
Is it a poisoned, solar kiss,
This peculiar phenomenon?
Cause for fear or celebration?

Scientific introspections
Talk of cirrus clouds on high
In which crystals of ice appear,
Which cause refractions and reflections.
No poison kiss as only I
Might posit. Nothing at all to fear.

And yet, to me, it does appear magical
Seeing the sun surrounded
Like this, imprisoned it would seem;
I'm glad it's nothing tragical
But still it has me enthralled and astounded
To see *Real* masquerading as *Dream.*

Sunrise, Sunset

Our home is on a long and narrow island,
One road wide.
People on one side glory in classic, open-sea sunsets;
We, on the other, prefer the brilliant surprises of dawn.
Sunrise is commencement, advent, beginning
Sunrise, looking forward, moving forward.
Sunrise for optimist; not the nostalgist.

I have exhorted before that any day whose sunrise I attend,
I own.
I modify that now to say: God still owns the day
But tenders me a conditional lease,
His terms both generous and exacting.
He will be with me through the new day, he vows,
And I, in return, shall never shy from acknowledging that.
I am free to do with the day as I will.
While acknowledging that His will trumps.

Swamp

"Swamp" is such an uncomely word
For some of earth's most fecund places,
Cauldrons of life, ancient, emerging.

We humans tend to denigrate
What we fail to understand.
What we fail to understand, we fear.
Swamps, we fear.

Part of it is words, what we choose to call such a place.
"Everglades" curdles.
Ah, but "River of Grass" as Ms. Douglas called it
Waves welcome.

A great photographer documents adoringly
The 'Glades, his subject and his home.
We look upon the grandeur of his images
Without fear,

Secure in their monochrome reflections
Of a world removed, somewhere else,
That cannot reach out and threaten us.

Swamps threaten.
They have beauty, true. But dare we risk the finding?
Does evil not there lurk?
There is silence we might covet if we did not cringe.
It is not what we see in a swamp that frightens,
But what we do not.
The enemy, not gator or snake
But our febrile imagination,
Our unknowing.

Robins

How mean taxonomists can be
As they make up names for friendly critters.
They use dead language to label the living
And try to be cute with the names they are giving.
I have to admit it gives the jitters,
Their taxonomic cruelty.

Take that most familiar of birds,
Spring's harbinger all glorious,
The robin. Bobbing for worms in the lawn,
Here today, come winter gone.
Turdus migratorious
They named him.
                        May they eat those words.

That Bird

Uncommon says the book
Here year 'round, not often seen
When seen, most likely not identified
Uncommon, unknown —

The me I yearn to be.

The Land of If's

I always wanted to visit the place I heard about somewhere:
Curious place; I *had* to go there.

A land, imagine, where nothing is certain or fixed.
Where everything lives between and betwixt,
Transient, always transitory,
Two endings written for every story
In this ambiguous land of conjecture
Where teachers must parent, with no time to lecture.
A land where all is always conditional,
Even the utterly non-volitional.
Where anyone can do anything *If*. . .
But *If* is a slope that leads to a cliff.
Follow an *If* and if you should stumble
You're in, you'll find, for quite a tumble.
Better be certain than take a chance,
Except here, as I said, *Certain* won't dance.
This is ambiguity's land,
Here doubt and duality make their stand.
And what do you think the land's Leader does
When he has to retire because, well, because?
When made to retire after many-a-year
Of telling each person what each wants to hear,
Defending *these* plans, decrying *those*,
Then defending *those* and decrying *these* --
Retired, what does he do, you suppose?
He writes *two* autobiographies.

How could one live in such a place,
Saying one thing to a person's face
Another when he's turned away?
Performing that ethical *tour jeté*.
Morality being whatever you say;
The wrong before is right today
Relativism, relatively okay
In the Land of *If's*, strange land somewhere.

When I tried to book passage to visit, I was told,
But sir, you're already there.

The News

I watch the news;
I see the killing,
The riots and the refugees,
The futile warriors of yesterday
Suffering today their toughest battles.
I see this. I hear this.
I take a walk.

The stream out back is rushing brown,
Engorged by the pelter of yesterday;
A "V" of honkers follows the familiar route through woods
The stream has carved over years.
A powder-puff flash of white bounds through the forest ahead,
While, timid but obedient, her fawn bounds after.
More deliberate are turkeys, three,
Strutting a slow animal path through maple and poplar.
Clinging to a stream-side hemlock trunk a red-headed woodpecker
Encodes all these stories and sends its dispatch.
Receiving it, I pretend that those stories alone are my news,
The only news I choose to heed today.

The Way Home

This is the road we used to travel,
Our happy way for thirteen years.
Whether padding a pathful of autumn consumed
Or strolling the corridor perfumed
By springtime lilacs in lavender tiers
On either side of the path of gravel;

Or sometimes slogging through snow to our knees
Towing a sled with needed supplies
From town across to our island retreat
Wishing that Browser would come down to meet
Us and pull the sled including his prize
That forty pound bag, he could do it with ease

But we'll drag the kibble and litter and loam
They'll owe us big, the cats and dog
We laugh as we tug along the sled
Our burden made light by the way we head,
For in snow or sun or dismal fog,
This is the path that takes us home.

The Winds in Me

I am a Christian
So I say
So I think
So I — but *do* I — believe?

Never does faith come easily
Never is commitment fixed

Today I believe
At least now, this morning while reading the Bible
I believe

But later this day?
Depends on what else
'Tween now and then
I allow to lumber my mind

Depends, too, on winds.
A fickle windsock am I
Moved by winds blowing many ways,
Any ways
And I am set awhirl

Believer?
Mock-believer? Make-Believer?
Certainly a Wanna-Believer?

But how can I make the whirling winds still?
Are they outside of me
Or in?

For the Wednesday of Holy Week

Today need we dread the approaching third?
When sounds the retributive thunder,
Trembles the earth and then is heard
The temple curtain torn asunder.

And the One who lived a life of love
Dies, convicted, loudly hated.
Innocence made victim of
A Devil's plotting, consummated.

Shall our retroactive dread arrest
Us on that stained and awful day?
No, because we know the best
News of all is on its way.

The next third day will bring the word
The world awaits to hear anew;
Each new year when springtime bird
Begins to sing softly to me and you

It's gentle hosanna . . . which quickly expands
To a chorus of creatures who loudly proceed
To shout and proclaim to all in all lands
He is risen. He is risen, indeed.

Three Friends

Three friends I know who all are blessed
With days fulfilled in most they do,
With talents amply recognized
With homes full of love and love requited
With lives on which has gently lighted
Grace by which they are baptized.
But do they know it? Only two.
The other has blessings like the rest

But when two offer a mealtime prayer
The other one may seem to ignore;
Not disdain and not repugn,
None of that. Too much sharing
Have they among them, too much caring
That one or two would never impugn
The religion or lack of the other or
Try to proselytize right there.

But isn't that what they're commissioned to do,
Proclaim the reason for their hope?
Share the love of the God above,
And when each moment of sharing arrives
They do it not with words but their lives,
Living God's glory, examplying His love
Agile as a phalarope
Committed as are all too few.

Unto Me

At first, I do not see her.
At second, I do not *want* to see her.
If I see her not, I need consider her not.
Ignoring protects me from getting involved,
Ignorance, my shield.

But no. She approaches,
As I wait in the line for the light,
The young woman I cannot ignore,
T-shirt and jeans, ragged,
Dirty face, empty,
Walks the line of cars ahead where drivers apparently also have shields.
Receiving no succor from them she homes intently on me
Clutching a scrawled slab of cardboard:
Out of work / Homeless / Please help
Directly outside my car, now,
She is looking at me.
I am not looking at her but I know she is looking at me.
Out of work.
Begging won't get you a job.
Homeless.
Why should I believe?
The world is full of scams and scammers.
Please help
I'd be a fool, a gullible fool.
Give her money for what? Drugs? Beer?
There are charities to help her likes.

Traffic is a caterpillar,
Accordioned shut at a stop;

But as now the light changes
This caterpillar begins -- so slowly -- to crawl,
Inching forward first its head segment,
Then, accordion extending, its mid segment drags along,
Then another and another
Until finally the stub -- me.

I am away.
Away from her,
Away from her beggary,
Away from the eyes I could not let myself see.
Away from all that . . .
But not, alas, from prickling thoughts.

Why was this the day our preacher chose that damning scripture?
....If you do it unto the least of these ... You do it unto me.
Whereupon, why did "One of the least of these" intercept me
homeward bound from church,
That conscience-haunting apparition challenging me?

Even if you would not see my eyes, hear my silent voice:
Who more needed those dollars you might have given, you or I.
Would you rather be living today in your life or mine?
Driving your comfy car
Or walking, re-walking my futile, humbling route?
Could you endure the indignity of a morning in the sun
Beseeching sightless eyes?
Of being, and having all know that you are, "One of the least..."?
Think on this. Enjoy your lunch.

I forego lunch and head straight upstairs to nap,
Perhaps to find peace.
Instead to find yet another voice, this a gentle voice whispering
Over and over, just two words,
Two curdling words . . .

                     . . . Unto Me.

War

Throughout ages numbered only by God
Have men — notice: not women but men — made war.
Wherever they were, whatever lands they trod
Were not enough. They had to have other or more.

They started to think of themselves as Ares or Mars
(For gods they surely deemed themselves to be)
Believing that war was destined in their stars,
 A biological necessity.

Thus, with sling and stone, arrow and bow,
Wielding sword and shield, mail and mace;
Or going fission, watching mushrooms grow;
They made earth a nervous-making place.

Wars of pride they were, and wars of greed,
Justified by those who were not just
As righteous, even Holy wars of need.
Can the cycle never end? It must.

Must we accept that wars are forever; peace a phantasm?
Do we have to accept if we do not want to believe?
Between war and peace — is there an unbridgeable chasm?
Is thinking that men might one day change naive?

Hail naivety!

Where Seas Cease To Be

I am drawn to those places where seas cease to be.
Not that seas do not agree with me.
But I prefer where reluctantly
They yield their dominion or have not claimed it yet. For me,
That is my favorite place to be.

I am a creature of land, made so by God,
Not sprung from conjectured progenitors washed in from sea,
No, please understand. I do not love water
For thinking that that's where kin used to be.

I love the sea for what it is and what it has.
Its freedom untrammeled; mysteries lying beyond
Its expanse, seemingly immeasurable,
   (And yet, playfully, some call an ocean "the pond."
It's temperament, unpredictable,
Now calm and soothing, now raging and furious.

Curious.

Wind

In the realm of a God we never see
We are blessed, we are cursed
From the very first
By something invisible as He

That which sustains our very being
Air, air
Everywhere
Working without our seeing

Oh, but we feel it, we do feel
The gentle ease
Of softening breeze
That a splintered soul can heal

In the woods, air can aid romance
As a zephyr stirs
The hims and hers
Of leaves, whose trees begin to dance

All delight from gentled air
But when air grows still
Unearthly still
That is the signal to beware

Time to prepare; to hurry, hurry
Soon winds will ravage
Storms will savage
With deadly cyclonic, tornadic fury

Then. Calm again. Be not chagrined
Know that the He
We cannot see
Remains still in control of wind

Worrying About Worrying

Sometimes I sense that I'm worried about something
But cannot remember what.
Whereupon, of course, I start to worry
That I do not know why I worry.

No More Words

I yearn now for an hour in the woods with no more words,
No word spoken *by* me, *to* me or overheard.
No word even thought or recalled.
I'll hike me the meadow out under an oak,
Put myself down on a pad of moss
At the foot of the tree, where, in springtime violets smile at me,
Lean back against the sturdy trunk
And what?
What can I do seated there without words?
I can sense, exercise all five:

Listen to sounds that are not words.
At least not words I know.
To chitters and scarfles,
Churbles, whispered grunts far off;
Someone is speaking to someones
But not to me. Those friends unknown must know
That I know only words.

Smell the wispy musk of woodland earth,
The aromatic blending of pine duff and last autumn's leaves,
Mingled on the ground underfoot; my footfalls exciting them.
It is the smell of death mingled with the promise of birth,
Which is to say, the perfume of life.

Touch the mosses. Run fingers over and through them.
Nature can be hard, in rock, in storm, in pummeling surf,
But mosses remind how gentle it can be to touch.
Indeed, is anything gentler? Down? The fuzz on a peach?
But having none here,
My touching fingers contentedly settle for moss.

Taste a sunwarmed raspberry plucked from its prickly vine,
Taste also, though — the air!
Savor the ineffable tonic of freshening breeze.
It has a smell, to be sure, but a taste as well.
And as it blows across my face, I imbibe.

See, then, the world of wonder that for this moment I inhabit.
I shan't catalog items: Tree, bush, grass and flower; too left-brain.
Instead, I shall ease my focus, blur my vision, till all I see merges
Into one amorphous collage of soft sensation.
Without words.

That is the worth of the exercise:
To sever our umbilical to words.
Too often, in the rest of our days and ways
Words strangle, asphyxiate, benumb us.
We are addicts, hopelessly hooked.

First thing awake: *Give us our vocables.*
Gotta to have words.
We turn on our word-spew machines,
Sometimes spewing pictures too but it's words we have to have.
We learn not to care what they mean,
Those words strung together by people unknown
Taken as friends because, like pushers,
They give us our fix.

Or we self-administer.
Someone — why, I do not know — calculated
That an average man utters ten thousand words a day.
Woman, that times two.
We narcotize ourselves with babbling,
Attempt to purge ourselves with ceaseless word-vomit.

And why?
We should know that our most important speakings
Need no words:
The smile that breaks at the sight of a love.
A firming hand taking supportive hold of one that trembles.
Lips upon lips.
One-two-three squeezes, soundlessly signaling *I-love-you.*
Even our language-less dog fluently restating the love he receives.

He is with me now in the woods,
Lying beside me 'neath the oak,
His soft ears being petted,
His blue-pool eyes gazing and adoring,

Wordlessly.

S. D. G.

www.ingramcontent.com/pod-product-compliance
Lightning Source LLC
Chambersburg PA
CBHW032140040426
42449CB00005B/331